A Drunk Mind
Meets
A Sober Heart

BY ERIS

A Drunk Mind Meets a Sober Heart

Copyright © 2025 by Eris.

MILTON & HUGO L.L.C.
4407 Park Ave., Suite 5
Union City, NJ 07087, USA

Website: *www. miltonandhugo.com*
Hotline: *1- 888-778-0033*
Email: *info@miltonandhugo.com*

Ordering Information:
Quantity sales. Special discounts are granted to corporations, associations, and other organizations. For more information on these discounts, please reach out to the publisher using the contact information provided above.

Library of Congress Control Number: 2025904607
ISBN-13:   979-8-89285-457-3   [Paperback Edition]
                  979-8-89285-456-6   [Digital Edition]

Rev. date: 03/07/2025

Contents

About the Book

A Drunk Mind Meets a Sober Heart is an intimate exploration of the human experience—raw, unfiltered, and unapologetically honest.

Inspired by the sudden loss of my father, this collection began as a journey through grief but evolved into something much greater. It delves into the complexities of love, heartbreak, self-discovery, mental health, and the quiet resilience that exists in all of us.

Each poem is a reflection of the tangled emotions that come with living and losing, healing and hurting. From the aching weight of loss to the bittersweet joys of connection, this book serves as a companion to anyone who has felt lost, broken, or unsure of their place in the world.

Through these pages, you'll find stories of longing, anger, courage, and hope—woven together with vulnerability and strength. It's a testament to the beauty of imperfection and the power of the written word to heal and connect us.

Whether you're grieving a loss, mending a broken heart, or simply searching for a mirror to your own struggles and triumphs, *A Drunk Mind Meets a Sober Heart* offers a sanctuary for reflection and understanding.

This book is more than poetry; it's a lifeline, a conversation, and a reminder that even in the darkest moments, you are never truly alone.

Dedication

To my father,
whose love and guidance shaped my world,
and whose sudden absence left an indelible void.

This book is my way of navigating the echoes of your voice,
the lessons you taught me,
and the pain of losing you so suddenly.

Each word is a fragment of the grief, love, and resilience
that you instilled in me—
a testament to the profound impact you had on my life.

Though you're no longer here,
your spirit lives on in these pages,
in the memories we shared,
and in the strength I find to keep going.

This book is for you—my guide, my hero, my father.
May these words honor the love you gave
and the legacy you left behind.

I. The Fragility of Love

Exploring the tenderness, beauty, and pain of relationships

Counterparts

I often viewed us as counterparts—
You, a child of the moon,
And I, a descendant of the sun.

Counterbalancing.
Cohesive.
Cooling and warming the world
Day by day,
Hour by hour,
Minute by minute.

A counterbalancing act of precision and chaos
We were a gallery of collective thoughts,
And a brilliant display of visualized emotions—
A completely discombobulated, orchestrated disaster
That somehow sank into a beautiful harmony
And melded

Perfectly.

We were us—
A total mess.
Far from perfection,
But perfect in a non-perfect way
In a perfectly imperfect world.

We were too much for the world to handle.

My Vision of Love

My vision of love changed the moment I met you.
Then it shifted again when I got to know you.
It's a fascinating thing—
You.
Me.
Us.

You became everything in my life
I didn't know I needed,
You became a test of my restraint,
A challenge to my sanity.

You and I were juxtapositions
Of the world's many ideals—
A daring and explosive combination
That left the world in flames
And the people breathless.

My vision of love changed the moment I met you.
We changed.
But we changed together,
And together, we burned.

We burned so brightly,
So hot,
So damn beautifully,
That we fell.

Like Icarus, whose wings were melted by the sun's truth, we fell,
Oh, darling, we fell hard,
And the crash was—
Well, it was catastrophic,
But I'd do it again.
For you.
For us.
I'd do it again.

What a vision we were

A Fickle Thing

Time—
It's a fickle thing.
Fate—
She's a tricky one.

But love?
My god, love is lethal.

It's a beautiful poison,
A delicious drug of ecstasy
That will take you higher,
And higher,
And higher—
Until you've gone so high
You can't even see the ground.
It'll take you so high
That reality becomes nothing more
Than a distant memory.

Love is another time and space—
And perhaps that's what he was.

A time.
A space.
A place.
A moment in the history of my life.

Yes, his words were honey,
And yes, his promises were sweet,
But in time, I'll come to see:
Love, as poisonous as she is,
Is a counter-agent to truth
And reality.

Love is a beautiful moment
That, when done right,
Can change your perspective
Into something other

That's the kicker though, we didn't do it right, and that, my dear,
is the unfortunate thing

Love is a very fickle thing.

Yes, Love Scares Me

Love scares me, and a gun doesn't.
It's a backward thought, isn't it?
That the bitter cold of a barrel
Against my skull frightens me less
Than the idea that you could love me.

The idea in it of itself is more fucked up than I care to explain
But, it is crazy to think that the caress of your soul
Against my own
Shakes me more than the kiss
Of a gun to my head.

Yes, love petrifies me, and a gun doesn't.
It's because love is more lethal
Than a gun—
A traitorous thing that is fleeting,
Deceitful.

It enters your life cloaked
In a pretty veil,
With a devastating smile,
And gorgeous lips that whisper
The most beautiful of hellos.

Love is a liar.
It hugs you tightly,
Pets you cutely,
Cuddles you nicely,
Then kills you slowly.

Yes, love terrifies me, and a gun doesn't.
It's because love infiltrates your mind,
Enters your soul and

Heals all the broken parts of you
You never thought could heal.
Then it smiles as it tears you apart again.

Love cheats on you.
Manipulates you.
It takes all the ways you've been hurt before
And does it again—
Bigger. Badder. Stronger.

It takes your heart,
Climbs it to its highest point,
Then drops it from a million miles up
Just to watch it crash on the pavement.

Yes, love horrifies me, and a gun doesn't.
It's because a gun makes its intentions known
From the start.
You see a gun, and there's only one thing
That crosses your mind—
You see a gun, and you know
The end is near.

A gun allows you to see it for what it is.
And a gun, a gun is honest.
It doesn't hide behind flowery words
And charmingly false intentions.

Yes, love scares me, and a gun doesn't.
Yes, love terrifies me, and a gun doesn't.
Yes, love frightens me, and a gun doesn't.

And yes, I'm well aware of the pain
Of dying from a gun wound,
But I'd rather die a million brutal deaths
Then be lied to once again.
Falling in love shouldn't make me bleed

And yet, it did.

9

The Moment We Met

From the moment we met, I understood,
without a shadow of a doubt, that catastrophe was at hand.
From the moment we met, I knew you'd ruin me, splendidly.
I realized you would reign over my heart.
I understood you would be the one to guide me,
Love me,
Care for me,
Infuriate me,
Confuse me, and so much more

For as long as I remain capable of discovering, of understanding,
the very being I am, I understand
You would be one of my many unexplainable paradoxes.
You were my beautiful disaster,
And I knew it from the start.

Called it

What Was It About Him?

"Why was he so important?" my friend asked.
I smiled sadly as I answered:
"You found your twin flame in her; I found my remedy in him.
I found light in his smile,
And laughter in his jokes.
I found happiness in his love.
I found myself with him again.
He healed a part of me I didn't think would ever be fixed.
I could look in the mirror again.
I could admit life wasn't so bad.
Our time, fleeting and incredibly short as it was,
Was a remedy to so much.

He was the first person who saw my scars.
He knew my trauma.
He showed me that there's strength in the history we come from.
He was strong, and he empowered me to be the same.
He was such a good friend.
His confidence was enrapturing.
He was annoyingly dickish.
Agony doesn't begin to describe my life right now.
With him, because of him, I became so much better.
He understood me, in a way no one ever had
Why I did what I did.
He understood why I became who I became.
He listened to me.
He allowed me to unapologetically display my hurt
And let me know it was okay; in turn, he showed me his.

Unfortunately, when he left, the cracks deepened,
And everything we healed shattered anew.

All that effort, wasted.

Stolen

You stole from me what I had just worked so hard to obtain—
Peace.
You stole the quiet moments I had fought so hard to find.
Like a wave,
Like a tide, you came, and when you left,
You took with you the remnants of an already battered heart.

Change

We don't see it, and sometimes we don't even know it,
But there are moments in our lives that slowly chip away
At the man, the woman, the people we are.
As time flies by, as days blur into months,
We realize now, we are not who we once were.

We blinked, and the people we once were are suddenly no more

The Night Before

That night before we said goodbye,
I knew something was wrong.
You hugged me tighter and longer than you ever had.
Your body was taut, and you couldn't really look me in the eye.

That night before we said goodbye,
there were many warning signs.
I saw the tension in your hands,
but I was too stupid
and too blind.

I think that night was my sign.
I could've made it right,
or maybe I couldn't have.
I think you had already made up your mind by then

That night before we said goodbye,
I knew something was wrong.
I think I just hoped differently
I had a lot of red flags.

The King of My Memories

You have become the king of my memories,
The reigning monarch of places we once roamed.
That park where we laughed—
Now a graveyard for our love,
Haunted by echoes of joy turned sorrow.

The Taco Bell down the street
Holds flavors of memories I can't digest.
I can't step inside without tears welling,
For we bared our hearts there,
And I can hardly bear the weight of remembrance.

In everything I do,
You linger like a shadow,
Constant reminders of our days and nights entwined.
Everywhere I look, there you are—
Your memory floods my mind,
And I wish it would relent.
I'd give anything to escape the thought of you
For even a minute.

The Symphony of Us

In the beginning, we were a duet,
notes soft and perfect,
timing flawless,
our rhythm syncing like breath.

Each laugh, a melody;
each touch, a harmony.
We composed a song only we knew,
unaware that every note
was leading us somewhere,
somewhere unknown.

Then came the dissonance—
a wrong chord,
an accidental silence,
and suddenly,
the music was harder to hear.

The world threw in its noise,
and we became two instruments,
struggling to play in tune.
I reached for your hand,
but it slipped away like a note lost in the wind.

Now, the symphony is a storm,
fingers clawing at the strings,
pounding the drums of what's unsaid.
We try to find our harmony again,
but the song we made
feels lost in the chaos we created.

Still, in every clash,
I hear a thread of us,
reminding me that,
maybe,
even in the chaos,
we were always music.

Our Story

Our story started with
"Once upon a time,"
But it didn't end with a
"Happily ever after."

I think that's what kills me

Letting Go

I realized that I loved you more than you could ever love me.
Then I understood that loving you should not kill me.
So I let go, hoping for the best,
Feeling the worst,
And regretting all the things we could've been.

A Hero's Death

I have a story to tell you.
It's a story that will make you wonder.
It's open to interpretation.
Interpret it as you may—
It stands as it will:

She could quote her favorite song
And let that tell her story.
She could scream her pain out loud
And then fall apart within.

Though—
Would her strength come into question then?
Would it be true
If she wished you the best
All the world could and would give?

Who knows?

Or—
Does she wish to have been the one to put you down under?
Will she be the one to drape your coffin
With a hero's flag,
Because for a time,
You were the one who saved her?

Will she be the one to mourn you
As she presses a final kiss to your lips,
Breaking the seal of a promise once made?

His death was unforgivable—
The cruelest of its kind.

And the murderer?

There are many suspects in question.

Jealousy denies it.
Infidelity claims its innocence.
Life suggests to look
Within the life of another.

Who holds the murder weapon?
Who planned the death of her hero
And executed it so well?

How about lies?
Misunderstanding?
A lack of trust?
Denial?

All hold merit.
All are suspects.
All hold reason.

You'll come to find
It was a collaborative effort—
A silent death,
And a brutal murder.

Each one slowly poisoned her hero,
And then her.

Our darling girl tells this story
From the grave—
Pale lips sealed shut,
Eyes wide open,
Forever stained
With the blood of broken promises.

She mourns you so

Tailored Love

In a world 8 billion strong,
you might think all the ways to love have been done.
Yet I can say with certainty,
the way I love you will always be unique.

For loving you isn't something someone else can replicate;
love you, loving me, the right way—
Is only something I can do.
I admire your strength,
cherish your heart—
these are gifts I hold dear,
an intimacy only I can nurture.

Because I will always love you
in a way tailored specifically for me,
crafted from our shared laughter,
woven through our quiet moments,
a love that remains unapologetically my own.

And while learning to love you, me, is not easy,
it is something I will strive to always do,
because I deserve love, too.

II. The Shadows of Loss

Delving into the heartbreak and grief that accompanies love and loss

Dead Corpse

I looked at you for the first time in months—
I mean, really looked at you.
Tears nearly spilled.
I think you saw the shock on my face;
I felt it too,
As my mask slipped away.
I couldn't hide my dismay,
My surprise,
My sadness.

What happened to you, my love?
You were so pale,
Eyes haunted,
Lips drained of color.
You looked utterly exhausted.
What happened to you, my love?
You seemed hollow,
Empty—
A walking shell,
Moving through life because you had to,
But hardly alive.

I had never seen a living corpse before,
And now,
You haunt my every step.

Falling for a Memory

I fell in love with a memory once,
Though I wasn't aware I had.
To fall in love with a memory
Is to dance on the edge of reality and fantasy,
Where echoes of laughter intertwine with whispered secrets.

The sun does indeed burn yellow,
With white halos at the edges,
A promise of warmth that betrays the chill of night.
And the sky, a vast canvas of blue,
Morphs with the whims of Mother Nature,
Painting storms and serenity in a single breath.

That is reality—cruel and beautiful.
Falling in love with a memory
Is like holding a flame that won't warm,
Its flicker a haunting reminder
Of the joy once felt, now just a ghost.
A blaze that illuminates the darkness
But leaves you cold, yearning for the touch
Of what was lost, slipping like sand through fingers.

I fell in love with a memory once,
And it loves me still, in its silent, haunting way.

I'm Sorry

I loved you for everything you were,
And I'm sorry
That wasn't enough.

I tried my best.

I Am Unsure Now

I am unsure
Whether I crave human company
Or the crushing weight of solitude—
The two at odds every day.

I am uncertain
If your presence in my life was a gift
Or a burden I never asked for.
If meeting you was something I needed
Or something I would have been better without.

I try to find the benefits
Of what you brought, but I seem incapable of doing
So I am left questioning—
If I could do it all again,
Would I?
Would I choose to smile,
To call you friend,
Or keep walking, ignoring you
As if you never existed?

Would I choose to be the woman I was,
Before you,
Or the woman I've become,
Because of you?

I'm unsure now
If the agony you've caused
Is worth the time I spent
Or if the uncertainty will ever stop killing me.

The Truth About a Broken Heart

The cruelest heartbreaks leave scars unseen,
It is pain that throbs, never leaving the heart—
A raw wound, never to be healed.
It is a love that's gone, tearing your soul apart,
Leaving you to face the bitter truth.

The memories of what could have been
Haunt you every day and through each night.
Dreams of love lie shattered, and then,
You're left alone to confront the bitter plight.

This heart of mine can't take the pain anymore

I Didn't Realize

I didn't realize
That the mention of your name
Would shatter me.

I didn't realize
That by simply uttering your name
My emotions could flip.

I didn't realize
Your absence would echo
In every room I entered,
Nor did I realize
That forgetting would hurt
More than remembering.

I didn't realize
That my carefully crafted tendril of happiness
Could morph into utter despair—
At the mention of you,
At the sight of you.

I didn't realize a lot of things.

Promise Me

When moonlight shines on a bitter night,
Promise my heart a gentle descent.
Promise me, as I linger on the edge,
You'll smile like you did at the start—
That smile, the one that made me fall.

All I am asking is that you don't make it hurt

What Did You Stand to Gain?

So, tell me—why did you do it?
What did you stand to gain?
Leaving me hollow, heart shattered,
With nothing left but pain.

I'm lying on the floor,
Crying my anguish away,
But I know it's my own fault—
I'm the one to blame.

I was foolish to believe
This time was not the same,
But he wasn't, in a sense—
He was different, unique,

Dark and handsome, with
A smile so serpentine,
His eyes were guarded, dangerous,
Yet his laugh—so beautifully disarming.

So, tell me, what did you stand to gain?

Why I Hate Promises

"I promise," he whispered.
My smile faltered, but I replaced it with a practiced grin.
I should have told him then and there,
But I didn't want to "ruin the moment."

I should have told him then and there—
I hate promises.
They're nothing more than pretty words,
Dressed up in lies,
Whispered sweetly,
Only to be broken.

I know; I'm a cynic.

A Hard Pill to Swallow

I have to let you go—
Not because you hurt me,
Not because you're bad for me,
But because you're the one person
I'll never truly have.

I fell in love with you,
Knowing from the start
Your love wasn't something I could hold.
Still, I stayed.
I stayed because having a part of you
Felt better than having none of you at all.

I told myself I could handle it,
That I could be happy with the way things are—
But I was lying.
Because every glance, every laugh,
Every moment that felt like more
Was a knife in my chest,
A reminder of what we'll never be.

I want to be the one you think of late at night,
The one you reach for when you're lost.
I want to be the girl you see
And can't imagine life without.

But I know I'm not her.
I know I'm just someone you care about,
But not in the way I ache for.
And no matter how much I wish it,
No matter how much I dream,
I'll never be more than this.

It kills me—
Quietly, slowly, in ways I can't explain.
But I can't let it consume me anymore.

Letting go doesn't mean I don't love you.
It means I have to choose myself.
I have to walk away,
Not because I want to,
But because staying will break me
In ways I can't fix.

It's the hardest truth I've had to face:
Some people aren't meant to be ours.
And sometimes, loving someone
Means knowing when to let them go.

The truth is a hard pill to swallow

I Was Already Broken

I was already broken when you met me.
Holding on to life by just a thread.
I was already dark, despising the very breath I inhaled

Happiness was a foreign concept to me.
Waking up happy every day—
A strange thing
Going to bed without a dark thought
Was a bliss I never thought I'd experience, that is until I met you

I didn't need you to break me.
I didn't need you in my life at all.

But I let you in.

I dropped my walls,
I dropped my guard.
I let you see
The most intimate parts of me.

And as a thank you—
You broke me more
Than I ever thought was possible

Seeing you hurts.
It angers me.

I mourn the loss
Of everything I could have had,
And everything I did have.

Why did you take the shattered pieces of an already fragmented
heart
And grind them to dust?

You had one job.

I Hate You

I love and hate everything about you.
What's everything, you may ask?
It's all of it.
I love the way you smiled when I said something stupid in
your car.
I love how you'd request a kiss and condition me to respond.
I love the marks you left on my neck, the bruises you left on my
soul.
I love how your eyes shone with tenderness just for me.
I love how you held me, kissed me, and buried your nose in my
neck.
I loved the way you entertained my bullshit, then called me out
on it.

I hate that after one night together, I couldn't sleep alone.
The touch of your skin ruined me.
I hate how your scent was the only thing that calmed me to sleep.
I hate how you watched me, your gaze so intense, it made me
shy away.
And I hated that I loved it.
When you called me "yours," it broke me.
That word—*mine*—ruined me.
In that moment, I felt *enough* for the first time in my life.

But do you know how bittersweet it is to feel enough
when you've spent your life feeling like you were never worth it?
I loved and hated everything about you—from the way you
checked in on me
to the flowers you gave me, wanting to replace them as soon as
they died.
I hated that you trusted me with your darkest parts,
and I loathe that you let me in.

I hate you,
but I still can't stop loving you.
I hate that you shut me out,
but I love how you've moved on.

I hate the lies, the cruelty of your words,
but I love how you made our time together the happiest of my
life,
even though the months after were the hardest.

I hate where I am now.
I hate how I've cried tears I promised myself I wouldn't.
I hate that you've claimed so many of my nights.
I hate that you've taken residence in my head.
I hate that I can't look at you without this overwhelming anger.

I hate you.

But I still love you.
I still worry about you, wish you the best.
I hate you, but more than that,
I hate what loving you made me.

I think you were one of my worst decisions

It Burns

Rage burns ever violently through my veins.
It's liquid heat—
It's liquid fire, and it burns.
It burns beyond any recognizable pain
That my body is aware of.

My gaze fixed upon your presence
Evokes such emotion in me
That it's almost paralyzing—
A paralyzing, confusing sacrilege.
It's an overdose on my senses.
Your presence makes me quiver,
And not in a good way.

Your brown eyes pull from the depths of my soul
The most bitter hatred,
And that ever-famous smile you once bestowed upon me that I
once loved
Stokes nothing but the raging hearth of pain.
Your scent sends me into a nauseating fit.

But I'll admit to you what I can't admit to anyone else:
I don't hate you.
The rage burns.
The anger boils
Yet beneath the fire of my hatred
Smolders the ashes of love I still hold.

Yes, seeing you pains me,
But I love you more now
Than I ever did then.
I miss you more than I ever thought I could.
It burns—
Make it stop.

Blood-Filled Insanity

One popular definition of insanity is,
"Taking the same action over and over again
And expecting different results."

So, was she insane, then, to keep searching?
To keep following wherever her desire led,
Even though after each encounter she was a bloody mess?

Laughing, clawing, blade in hand,
She carved into bitter, pale flesh
The one desire she could never have.

It taunted her—
Hourly.
Daily.
Monthly.
Yearly.

Head banging against a wall—
Each hit a dent—
A dent into the wall,
A dent into her mind,
A dent into her soul.

Laughing. Clawing. Blade in hand.
She carved into bitter, pale flesh
The one desire she could never have.

One popular definition of insanity is,
"Taking the same action over and over again
Expecting different results."

So, was she insane, then,
To keep searching,
To keep following the desire of her heart?
To keep searching for... love?

Desperation makes us do silly things,
But sometimes, it makes us bleed.

In Another Universe

In another universe,
I think we could have been better than this.
Where our words were softer,
Our silences kinder,
And the weight we carried
Didn't break us,
But bound us closer.

There's a version of us out there—
Whole, unfractured,
Where time didn't steal what we couldn't repair,
And love was enough.

But not here.
Here, we are a story
Of almost and if-only,
A constellation that never quite aligned.

And the what ifs are what keep me up at night.

The Things We Don't Say

I probably should have told you
That I loved you
One more time.

Now I'll never get the chance,
And silence remains my punishment.

The Way You Treat Me

I love the way you treat me like a stranger,
as if those countless hours spent learning my heart
and mapping the contours of my mind
were not something you took pride in.
As if you don't know me at all.

Perhaps we were always strangers,
because you hurt me as if you never knew me,
as if tearing my heart apart
was nothing to you,
meant nothing to you.

You Broke me

You broke me like a forgotten promise,
Like something you intended to care for
But grew too lazy to look after.
You broke me like something you got too clumsy
To keep safe, too tired to love.
You broke me like a promise you forgot,
A care you lost, a love you left behind.

My Failed Attempt

As you watched my heart shatter
And along with it, the woman you knew,
You told me,
"Don't let this stop you from loving again."
I shook my head,
Because I think you'd forgotten—
You had been my 'loving again.'

You had been my 'let me try once more.'
And in that effort,
I broke beyond repair.

You were a failed attempt

If I Could Break You

If I could break you
The way you broke me,
I would.
Only then would justice
Finally be served.

The Reality

The reality of it all is that
No one will love me the way I long to be loved.
No one is capable of loving me as I deserve.
No one will love me as I need—
Not even myself.
'Tis a sad, sad life.

Wasted Love

Loving you was such a waste of time.
We could have stayed strangers,
avoiding this mess we made—
Now look at us, lovers turned enemies.

Now when I see you, I laugh—
at you, at myself, at us,
at the history we share.
It's ridiculous, really,
how we could have kept it simple,
but instead, we jumped in,
only to crash and burn in a month.

We could have stayed strangers,
kept our distance.
Instead of rushing into something
that fell apart so quickly,
leaving us with nothing but the bitter taste
of what we tried to build.

I don't know whose time was wasted more, yours or mine?

Just One of Those Things
They Used to Tell Me

I remember when you'd say,
"I brought you into this world, and I can take you out."
At nine years old, those words were stones in my chest,
Heavy, sharp, and cold.

I remember how much they frightened me,
How they carved shadows into my nights,
Leaving me wide-eyed and searching
For the mistake I made to earn them.

I remember thinking,
What if you didn't want me?
What if you didn't love me?
What could I do to make that change?

Now, I look back,
And I wonder if you remember those words,
If you know how they echo even now.
And in the quiet, I find myself whispering,

"Do it.
Put me out of my misery.
Do what nine-year-old me,
Twelve-year-old me,
Sixteen-year-old me, and
Nineteen-year-old me
Were too afraid to do."

Because sometimes, it feels like
You brought me into this world,
Only to teach me how to suffer in it.

A Letter to My Best Friend

I didn't see it at first.
Your smiles still came, though smaller.
Your laughter, softer—more fragile.
You wore your pain well,
Hiding the cracks where the light once lived.

I missed the signs—
The long pauses,
The forced cheer in your voice,
The weight behind your words
That I didn't question soon enough.

But then I saw it.
Your mask slipped, and there you were—
Broken, struggling,
Each breath heavier than the last.

I saw the shadow of what they'd done,
The anger you swallowed,
The betrayal that lingered like an open wound.
I saw the fight leave you,
And it hurt to watch someone so strong crumble.

I should've caught it sooner.
I should've asked, should've known.
I'm sorry for not being there
When you needed someone the most.

But I'm here now,
And I'm not going anywhere.
You're my friend, my brother, my anchor,
And I'll stay until the storm quiets.

Even the strongest break sometimes.
And when you do,
I'll catch you—
Every single time.

Pain & Brutality

It's not the kind of pain you can scream away,
Not the sort you can bury under a blanket of numbness.
It's the type that seeps through your veins,
A quiet assault that leaves you breathless,
And yet, it never really stops.

Brutality isn't always blood,
Sometimes it's the way your own mind betrays you,
The thoughts that carve into your skin,
The words you never said,
The silence that roars louder than any shout.

It's the feeling of holding a broken piece of yourself
And knowing it'll never fit back the way it was.
Pain is more than just feeling shattered,
It's the awareness that you'll never be whole again,
And the brutality is knowing that the world
Doesn't stop for your destruction.

III. The Unsaid Truths

Confronting Hidden feelings and the weight of what is left unsaid

Grief's Echo

I think I lost more than just you that night.
I lost the trust I once had in myself,
The certainty that I could stand tall without breaking.
I lost pieces of who I was,
The fragments of me scattered in the wake of your absence.

I think grief is quiet at first,
A murmur that grows louder the longer you ignore it.
But tonight, it was deafening.
The weight of your silence crushed me,
And I wonder if I'll ever be able to breathe again without it.

I think I became smaller,
As if the grief had worn me down,
Carving into my bones,
Shaping me into someone I don't recognize.

I keep looking for you in the spaces between my thoughts,
Hoping you'll return to fill the emptiness,
But all I find is the hollow echo of what was.
And I wonder how to stop chasing a ghost,
When the real loss is the person I've become.

A Held Breathe

I have yet to understand
how, in a single moment, you went from being my reality
to just a memory.

A year later, I still can't comprehend
how within one breath,
you shifted from my present to my past.

Time doesn't exist—
it's just a cruel illusion I can't shatter,
no matter how desperately I try to reach through it,
just to have you back.

Losing you has destroyed me
in a way I'll never recover from.
I never thought I'd be speaking of you as a memory,
never thought I'd have to say you "used to,"
because "doing" isn't something you can do anymore.

Losing you was brutal—
sudden, jarring,
a world pulled out from under me, tilted on its axis,
and nothing has righted since.

Your last breath became the breath I held,
and I'm still holding it—
afraid that if I exhale,
it'll mean letting go of the last piece of you
I've been clinging to,
and I'm not ready for that.

I am so scared to let go

The Prison of Grief

In a world that moves forward,
you might think grief is something that passes.
Yet I can say with certainty,
the way it holds me is relentless, and unforgiving.
For grief isn't something time can wash away;
it clings to me, binding me tight—
an echo only I can hear.

I wake, and it seems like the day has started again.
I wake, and I can hear you dying across the room—
the ragged pull of breath, the silence that follows.
It echoes in my chest, filling the hollow,
a space once held by hope, now haunted by that sound.

I'm transported back to the moment when time stood still,
when the world splintered into shards,
each sharp enough to pierce my heart.
I relive your strangled gasp,
the way your eyes turned glassy and far away,
searching for a peace I couldn't give—
a peace I could only witness, never offer.

Every breath I take pulls me deeper,
a prisoner to the memory,
a captive to the past.
My grief is my prison, my mind the iron bars of my entrapment.
Thoughts coil and tighten like chains,
binding me to that final moment.

The day ends, but it doesn't really end.
Night falls, but it brings no rest.
Sleep is just another realm where shadows replay the same
tragedy.

I wake, and the cycle begins again.
I am locked in this relentless cage,
every dawn is a return to loss,
every heartbeat carries the echo of your last.

The Five Steps I Can't Escape

They say that grieving is a five-step process:

First, you deny.
Then, anger sets in.
Next comes bargaining.
After that, the weight of depression.
And finally, acceptance.

They say grief is unique for everyone,
that it's a process you walk through alone.
They say grieving isn't linear.
I agree.

But what they don't tell you is that grief can become a trap—
that sometimes, you get stuck.
And once you're stuck, getting unstuck becomes almost
impossible.

I watched my savior, my protector, my first love,
take his last breath in my arms.
I was powerless, helpless, frozen,
and now I relive that day over, and over, and over again.

Denial holds me there:
I relive the 911 call, thinking, *This can't be real.*
I relive the anxious wait, the drive to the hospital,
repeating to myself, *You're fine—you're going to be fine.*

Anger fills the silence that follows,
rage at the unfairness, at life, at myself for not being able to
save you.
I want to scream at everything I can't change.

Bargaining comes in whispers to a god I never believed in,
a silent promise: *If you give him back, I'll do anything.*
I remember walking through that hospital lobby,
repeating it like a mantra,
as if I could still somehow rewrite the end.

Then depression drowns me, its weight like lead.
I relive the doctor's words, the nurse's regretful gaze,
and the pitiful looks from strangers who know I've lost
something irreplaceable.
I can feel myself sinking, unable to resurface.

And acceptance—
I'm told it's supposed to come like a quiet release.
But I'm still waiting.
Because we both went into that hospital, but I never left,
and I don't know how to move forward without you.

So I remain there, suspended in that moment,
stuck between the stages, caught in that breath,
reliving you in fragments,
each memory both a comfort and a prison.

Took Two

They took two things from me—
my name and my silence.

They called me strong,
but it felt more like surrender.
They called me brave,
but it felt more like pretending.

Grief didn't ask—
it demanded.
It hollowed me out,
then handed me a mask
I didn't ask to wear.

I became two people—
the one who smiles
and the one who screams in secret.
The one who moves forward
and the one who still waits.

No one saw the fracture,
only the frame that held it.
No one heard the echo,
only the words I forced out loud.

They took two things from me—
my name and my silence—
and left me with a voice
I'm still learning how to use.

Death took two that day

A Love I Keep Shelved

Some days, I feel like a terrible daughter,
because your urn sits hidden in my closet, collecting dust.
Not because I don't love you, or because I'm ashamed to have
you out in the open,
but because seeing it—seeing you—forces me to confront a
reality I still can't accept.

In my mind, you're still alive, still laughing, still here.
So I keep the urn out of sight, as if hiding it could keep that
image intact.
I tell myself it's just for now, just until I'm ready.
But every time I reach to open the closet door,
that weight presses down, and I close it again,
locking the truth behind that door, keeping it just out of reach.

I wonder what you'd say if you knew—
if you'd understand that I'm not ready to lose you,
that I'm still running from the truth, clinging to the echoes of
your voice,
pretending that any day now, you'll walk back into the room.

Forgive me if I can't face it, if I leave you there, unseen.
Because the day I bring you out into the light,
is the day I have to admit you're really gone.

I'm not ready to face the truth, I hope you're okay with that

Following Suit

I almost followed suit after you that day.
I wanted to mirror your glassy-eyed stare,
your lack of breath.
I wanted my heartbeat to match yours—
still.

"Be still, my beating heart," they say.
I wished for that, that day—
to silence the storm inside,
to numb the ache that lingered long after you were gone.

Even now, on nights when the stars hang low,
and the moon glows gentle against painted black,
I still wish for it—
to be as cold as you,
to feel nothing at all, to escape the weight of this pulse in my
chest.

But the truth is—
I didn't stay because I wanted to.
I stayed because I had no other choice.

Because the day you died,
I realized there was so much left undone—
unfinished words,
fractured dreams,
empty spaces only I could fill.

Like Hamilton, standing in the ruins,
I felt the weight of time pressing forward.
I couldn't stop it.
So I let it carry me,
even as my knees buckled under its burden.

I wanted to leave with you that day,
to slip into the dark without a trace,
to find peace in the stillness you now own.

But here I remain,
alive in a world that no longer feels like mine,
haunted by your silence,
but driven by the echoes you left behind.

I carry the weight of breath,
not because I wanted to—
but because I had to.

Because there is so much left to do.

Stupid Wish

Stupidly enough, there's a part of me that wishes
you had been a deadbeat dad,
just so losing you didn't hurt the way it does.
It would make grieving so much easier,
turn my heartache into something I could fight against,
a reason to be angry instead of just lost in sorrow.

I could scream at the man who chose to walk away,
blame him for the empty chair at the table,
for the laughter that will never fill the room again.

But, I can't, because I am one of the fortunate ones, you stayed
So, instead, I'm haunted by the good memories,
by the love you gave, the way you held me close,
and that makes it all so much harder.

How do I reconcile this pain?
How do I grieve for someone who loved me so deeply
yet left me with this unbearable weight?
I want to shake the world and make it understand,
but all I have is this ache— the longing for clarity in a mess of
emotions.

If you were flawed, if you had walked away,
maybe then I could bury this hurt with a sense of closure.
But here I am, caught in the middle,
struggling to make sense of a love
that's both my greatest joy and my deepest pain,
wondering if I'll ever be able to let go.

The Comfort of the Past

I realized that living in the past
is so much easier than living in the present,
or even imagining the future.
There's a warmth,
a certainty,
in staying there.
Things don't change in the past;
they've already happened,
and you know how they end.

For someone scared of the unknown,
the past is the perfect place to hide,
safe from the unpredictable chaos
of what's to come,
and the uncertainty of now.

It's okay to visit the past,
to sit there for a moment,
to remember the warmth,
the comfort it gave you.
But don't stay there.
Don't let yourself become part of the past
you love to visit so much.
Because once you do,
no one can get you out— not even you.

I'll miss you if you don't come back.
You belong in the present,
with all its mess and potential.
Please, don't get lost in the past.
There's still time left here.

The Holidays Without You

You know what I didn't expect to change so sharply
when you left?
The holidays.

As Thanksgiving creeps closer,
I find that what I do have to be grateful for
escapes me.
It's overshadowed by your absence,
your empty seat at the table,
the silence where your laughter used to fill the room.

There's a side of me that minimizes things.
It whispers,
"Stop being selfish.
You have so much to be grateful for."
It scolds me for feeling ungrateful,
even though, yes,
I've lost someone who meant the world to me.

But then there's another side—
the side that aches for you.
It tells me I have every right to feel this way.
That no amount of blessings
could ever measure up to what I've lost.
To who I've lost.

During a holiday meant for giving thanks,
I don't know how to.
I don't see much to give thanks for.
And then there's Christmas.
The lights seem dimmer this year,
the carols sound hollow.
Even though this is the first year
I've felt like putting up a tree since Mom left,
the act feels bittersweet.
The tree stands heavy,
laden with memories instead of ornaments.

You never cared much for Christmas—
but somehow, you brought it to life anyway.
Your quiet presence added something
I never noticed until now.

Without you,
the season feels empty,
as though its magic left with you.

The holidays aren't the same.
They're quieter.
Colder.
Lonelier.

I don't know how to celebrate when your absence
is louder than any cheer.

Your Last Words

The last words you said to me were,
"Goodnight, I love you. I'll see you tomorrow."
Simple. Familiar. Safe.
I wish I knew then
what I know now—
that tomorrow would never come,
that those words would echo endlessly
in the quiet of my nights,
a bittersweet comfort
and a sharp reminder
of what was lost.

If only I had held on tighter,
memorized the sound of your voice,
the way those words felt
as they wrapped around my heart.
But how could I have known?
Tomorrow always felt certain—
until it wasn't.

God, if only I had known

Angry Rant

Fuck you for leaving me the way you did.

I don't actually mean that,
but damn, it's hard not to feel it sometimes.

You were supposed to be my anchor,
the one I could always count on.
I was not supposed to be doing this without you.

I know you didn't mean to go,
that life doesn't always give us a choice,
but it doesn't change the fact that I'm angry—
angry at the situation, angry at you,
and mostly angry at myself for feeling this way
when all I wanted was for you to stay.

There it is:
the anger in my grieving process.

The Shape of Grief

Grief isn't loud.
It doesn't scream or shatter glass.
It seeps in—
quiet, patient—
and rearranges the furniture of your soul.

It moves things around
without asking,
turns lights off
and leaves doors open.

Grief isn't sharp.
It dulls everything—
edges, colors, sounds—
until the world hums in gray.

It lives in the spaces
between breaths,
in the pause before you speak,
in the weight of words
you decide not to say.

Grief isn't cruel.
It's just heavy.
It doesn't crush you all at once—
it settles in,
makes itself at home,
and waits.

And maybe that's why
it never leaves.

Because grief isn't death.
It's survival.
It's learning to carry the weight
without letting it sink you.

It's letting the ghosts stay,
but refusing to let them
own the room.

Misery

They say the world is ending,
But I couldn't care less.
I stopped paying attention;
I can't fear that finality anymore.
For me, the world ended
The moment you said goodbye.
So I say, let it end.

Living Despite the Pain

I'm learning to laugh through the pain,
To crack a grin even while I'm breaking.
Because the world didn't stop when your breath did,
And it didn't stop when mine faltered, either.

So I gather the shards of my shattered days,
Searching for the light that hides in the shadows.
Even though it hurts,
I try to find the good in the dark.

It's what you would have wanted.

All I hope is I'm making you proud while I do it

Echoes to the Stars

You told me you'd always be there for me,
And I imagined it would be as you were.
Now I've learned it may mean as you are, too—
I don't really know.

I'm just hoping that when I speak to the stars,
My voice echoes to you across the skies.

The Worst Part

They don't tell you what the worst part of grief is.
They don't tell you that when someone dies,
a part of you dies too.

They don't tell you the funeral is for two—
that you're not just burying them,
but also the person you were
before the world caved in.

They don't tell you that grief
isn't just missing them—
it's mourning the version of yourself
that existed when they were still here.

There's a lot they don't tell you.
And I wish they had.

It Comes in Waves

It comes in waves—
some days are good,
others are bad.
Some days I can smile,
while other days I can't stop crying.

Some days, things don't seem so bad,
and other days,
my anger surges like a storm,
scaring even me.

Some days, I laugh hard,
freely, unburdened,
while other days,
I feel like life is moving on without me.

Some days I die inside,
mourning you as if it's the first time,
and other days, I'm just silent,
lost in the chaos of it all.

It's a constant fluctuation,
this rollercoaster of emotion,
and I'm so damn tired of it.

The highs and lows twist,
like a relentless ride that won't stop
when all I want is off.
The good times outshine the bad,
but the bad can't compare to the good—it doesn't end.

How do I keep fighting this
when it feels like I'm losing myself?
I just want to find a moment of peace,
but all I get is the echo of your absence,
a reminder of what was,
and what will never be again.

In Search of Your Voice

I've had to make so many hard decisions since you've been gone,
and I don't know what I'm doing.
I try to do things that will make you proud,
walk a path that justifies all the hard work you poured into me,
but honestly? I don't think I am.
Every choice feels like a weight,
each step taken in uncertainty,
and I wonder if you'd even recognize me now.

There are so many moments I could have used your guidance,
your encouraging words that always seemed to light the way.
But now?
Talking to the stars just isn't cutting it anymore.
I search for your face in the night sky,
hoping for a sign, a whisper of wisdom,
but all I feel is the cold void where you used to be.

So, I don't know what to do.
Adulthood is hard,
and I don't know that I'm doing it right.
Every day feels like a balancing act,
with decisions piling up like a mountain,
each one heavier than the last.
I'm fumbling in the dark,
grasping for answers that slip through my fingers.

I wasn't ready to do this without you,
to navigate a world that feels so much larger now,
so much scarier.
I want to make you proud,
but it's hard to move forward when
all I want is to turn back time,
to hear your voice guiding me,
to feel your hand on my shoulder,
telling me it's going to be okay.
But instead, I'm left with echoes,
and all I can do is keep searching for a way to honor you
in this life that feels so lost without you.

It's Cold Tonight

It's cold tonight.
The temperatures have dropped.
The winter coats are out,
Even though it's only 65 degrees.
But you know us Floridians,
Pulling out scarves at anything under 80.

You would have laughed,
Told me you've experienced temperatures in the negatives,
That this was nothing—
How you'd willingly go live in the middle of cold-as-fuck Alaska
like a lunatic.

And I remember, I'd laugh each time you'd tell me that story.
I'd look at you crazy—
Because who honestly wants to go live in -40 degrees willingly?
I'll be honest, I miss that story.
Could use it right about now.

I wonder if your heaven has you out there,
Laughing at the cold,
Building your home in the frost and snow.
I can see it now—
You, undaunted by the chill,
Making the cold your companion,
Turning the frost into warmth with that wild grin of yours.

I wonder if you still think of me,
If my face lingers in your thoughts like you used to linger in mine.
I wonder if you'd laugh at the way I pull on my jacket
Even when it's only 65 degrees.
I can feel the weight of the cold tonight,
But it's nothing compared to the emptiness in my heart,
The kind of cold only your absence can bring.

But maybe, just maybe,
Wherever you are,
You're still laughing—
Still braving the cold with that same fire in your soul.
And in that warmth,
I find a piece of you to carry with me
Through the long nights ahead.

Left in the There

I left you behind in 2023,
A place where shadows breathe
And echoes refuse to fade.
When the clock struck twelve
And the world stepped forward,
You stayed—
Rooted in the there,
In a year that no longer belonged to me.

I crossed into 2024 alone,
Each step a quiet rebellion
Against the weight of your absence.
The air was sharp with beginnings,
Yet the hollow where you once stood
Clung to me like a second skin,
Unseen, but undeniable.

Did you choose to remain?
Or was it the world that unraveled you,
Leaving only fragments
Too fragile to carry forward?
I asked the night for answers,
But all it offered
Was silence shaped like your name.

Still, I move.
Through days you will never know,
Through moments untouched by your memory.
I carry you in the spaces between breaths,
In the quiet ache of what was,
And the bittersweet hope
Of what lies ahead.

A Legacy, Unspoken

On one of my many trips to the storage unit,
I found your shadow box—
The dust settled softly on its surface,
But the medals and ribbons inside still gleamed, as if new.
I stared at the box,
The weight of it heavy in my hands,
And cried.
The remnants of your legacy felt like a phantom in my grip—
A life lived in service, now just memories.

You served your country well,
And no one will ever truly know what you gave.
I am the daughter of a hero—
A man who willingly sacrificed everything for millions of lives,
And yet, for all the lives you saved,
Your name remains unspoken by most.

But I remember.
I am one of the fortunate ones,
The one who got you back,
So you could continue to live, with me.

And you lived.
You lived for many glorious years,
Each year a testament to your strength,
To the resilience you carried inside,
Even when your body grew weary.
You fought, not just for your country,
But for what was right, for what was good,
For me,
For yourself,
For Mom,
For your son.
You lived not for the world, but for us,
For the people who mattered to you most.
And with every fight,
You built a legacy that could never be erased—
A legacy that still stands,
But now, it stands with me.

It was in your nature to fight.
To never give up,
To never back down.
And you did, until your very last breath.
You served your country well,
And in that service, you shaped our lives.
Now, your peace is earned,
And though you're gone,
Your legacy lives on,
As long as I breathe,
As long as I carry your story,
Your fight,
Your love for your family.

The battle is over,
But I will continue the fight for you.

IV. The Phoenix Within

Reclaiming power, healing, and self-worth

The Villain

In someone else's story,
You're the villain.
The bad guy,
The toxic ex,
The fake best friend.

Even though you did nothing
But right by them,
You're still the shadow they point to,
The name they curse in the dark.

And sometimes,
You just have to learn to be okay with that.
Because if there's one thing I've learned,
It's this:

No matter how loud you yell
Or how softly you explain,
The truth won't matter—
Not to them.

They've written you in ink,
Carved you into the role they need you to play.

Believe me, I know it sucks.
But you can't rewrite someone else's story.
You can only let go
And keep living your own

The Stigma of the Unspoken

I've realized how people cower
At the mere mention of suicide.
They recoil from the conversation,
Quick to toss out platitudes like,
"No, you shouldn't do that,"
"Don't think like that,"
Or, my personal favorite:
"I could never. It means giving up."

And in those words,
Do they realize what they're saying?
The unspoken undertones of judgment,
The accidental pedestal they place themselves upon.

It gives off this air of elitism,
This sense of moral high ground,
As if they're too lofty, too pure,
To ever stoop to such a place of despair.

As if to break, to surrender,
Is to betray their humanity.
As if those who do
Are lesser, weaker, unworthy.

And I suppose that means they are lucky,
Fortunate to never feel their world collapse,
To never be swallowed whole by the weight,
Unable to see any light above the waterline.

Lucky to never reach the point where "toughing it out"
Means gritting your teeth through unending agony—
Until the toughness itself fractures,
And there is no toughness left.

Perhaps, in a sense,
They are the elite—the fortunate ones—
Blessed to have never faced such darkness.

But do not, for one second,
Mistake their luck for superiority.
Do not, for one second,
Dismiss the survivors and fallen alike.

For to face the unthinkable
Takes a strength they may never understand,
A courage that remains unseen,
A battle that echoes in silence.

The survivors are warriors. And the fallen?
They were, too.

It's Fine

My therapist says I have a catchphrase:
"It's fine."
She says I wield it like a shield,
An armor for everything wrong in my life.

Someone hurts me.
"It's fine."
A day at work—absolute hell?
"It's fine."
Feeling abandoned, unloved?
"It's fine."

She asks me why,
Why those two words sit
On the tip of my tongue,
Why I cling to them
Like a lifeline tied to nothing.

I just shrug.
Because it is.
Because breaking down feels selfish.
Because crying won't fix what's already broken.

The truth is:
"It's fine" means it's not.
It means I'm tired of explaining.
It means I don't want to be seen.
It means I've been strong for too long,
And I can't afford to shatter.

So I say it again,
"It's fine,"
And hope no one notices
How much I want to be saved.

Unlearning the Apology

I have to learn how to stop saying sorry
for the things I can't control.
I apologize even when it isn't my fault,
as if it's somehow my responsibility,
as if my voice has to shrink to fit others' expectations.

It's automatic—
a reflex,
like a breath I don't think about until it's too late.
I have to unlearn that behavior,
to stop shrinking every time I speak.

With every apology, I seem to make myself smaller,
as if my worth is tied to others' comfort,
as if my presence needs to apologize for existing.

I have to stop making myself small
just to make others feel bigger.
I have to stop saying sorry
for things that are out of my hands,
and start learning how to stand tall in my own truth.

The Things Said

The things said in the "heat of the moment"
Last longer than the moment itself.
They remain burned into my subconscious,
A new record playing on repeat.
With each repetition, the words cut deeper,
Until they become the new background noise of my life.
They echo in my mind,
Like a song I can't stop playing.

Letter to My Inner Child

Dear darling girl,

It's been a while.
I've heard you knocking on my door,
but I'm sorry I haven't dared to answer until now.
Like you hesitated to knock on Mommy and Daddy's door,
fearing you'd bother them,
I've hesitated, scared of what awaits on the other side.
It's been too long. I almost don't know what to tell you.

Why were you so scared to knock?
You thought you were a bother from a young age,
and that thought lingers still.
Don't you know you're deserving of help and comfort?
You can't face the world alone, baby.
Asking for help doesn't mean you're weak;
it makes you human.

I'm sorry I didn't answer sooner.
I've been busy trying to keep us together.
I realize no one will apologize for your wrongs,
so I will, on behalf of them.

I apologize for your broken heart,
for Mommy not staying,
for Daddy changing,
for every day coming home from school feeling like a hassle.
I'm sorry home stopped feeling like home,
for being a pawn in a game you didn't know you were playing.
I'm sorry you were never really a child,
that they called you sensitive,
that you weren't treasured like you should have been.

I'm sorry your self-worth was questioned in the fifth grade,
for being taught to tolerate disrespect to keep friends,
for thinking letting those racist jokes slide was okay,
for not knowing your worth.

I'm so sorry you couldn't see your own reflection with love,
that you were harsh to yourself,
that you couldn't feel the beauty within you.
You are such a beautiful girl,
growing into a powerful woman.

It wasn't your fault.
Their breaking up wasn't your fault.
They had issues they didn't handle well,
and you were caught in the crossfire.
You were never anyone's first choice,
and I'm sorry you haven't been your own,
for being pushed to that point.

I'm sorry for every time you stared at a pill bottle,
wondering how many it would take to not wake up,
for thinking about a gun,
for looking at a knife,
wondering how deep to cut,
for deeming yourself worth only your body.
I'm sorry you couldn't love your body,
that you couldn't see the brilliance in your life
or the beauty of your magnificent mind.

I'm so sorry no one taught you how to love yourself,
that you tore yourself down to fit into their confinement,
that you didn't have the energy.

I love you.
You are enough.
You always have been;
you never had to prove yourself to anyone but yourself.
But as a Black girl in America,

the world is dangerous,
and as a Black woman,
the world is not your friend.
I'm sorry every day you're on defense,
that you don't believe in love anymore,
that they tore your heart apart and left it in shreds.

It's not your fault.
It was never your fault.
You are who you are, and that's beautiful,
perfect.
Your eyes are endlessly stunning,
your smile, gorgeous,
your teeth, perfect,
your body, ravishing,
your mind, breathtaking.
Everything about you is just as it should be.
Nothing must change unless you wish it to.

I'm sorry you're not in your best place.
Hey, darling girl, I've heard you knocking for a while,
and I didn't have the heart to answer.
But I'm here now, and I'll answer from now on,
every single knock.

Sincerely,
Future you

Admittance

Admitting you're wrong
Won't kill you.
Stop acting like it will.

Advocacy

Today, I chose myself.
Not softly, not timidly—
but loudly, like a thunderclap
that demanded to be heard.

I stood in the storm of expectations
and let the rain wash away
everything that wasn't mine to carry.

I didn't shrink.
I didn't apologize.
I didn't barter my worth for scraps of affection.

I said no.

Not because it was easy,
but because it was necessary.
Not because I wanted to fight,
but because I finally knew
I was worth fighting for.

I chose myself today—
not as an afterthought,
not as a backup plan,
but as the main event.

And maybe they'll call it selfish.
Maybe they'll call it pride.
But I'll call it what it is—
survival.

Canvas of Despair

I wanted to paint the stars with my tears,
Instead, I painted the world with my hatred,
Colored it with my despair,
And yearned to burn it with my anger.

My Own Savior

I'm so proud of myself
for surviving,
when all I wanted was to die.
I made it.
I did it.
And no one can tell me shit.

I am strong, even when I cry at night.
I am powerful, even in my manic moments.
I lived when every ounce of me wanted to die.
Damn, I'm so proud of myself.
Damn, I'm good.

Thank You

I never said thank you,
not in a way that feels like it matters.
You held me together when I couldn't,
your hands steady when mine shook.
You watched me drink my pain away
and silently passed me the bottle,
knowing that, for a moment,
it was all I had.

Even though you never truly understood,
you sympathized,
never judging, just being there—
a quiet strength beside me in the dark.
When I was lost in my own mess,
you were the only one who seemed to know
how to keep me from falling apart completely.

I need to tell you thank you—
for showing up,
even when I couldn't show up for myself.
For seeing the part of me I couldn't see,
the piece of me that was still worth saving,
even when I had nothing left to give.

It's not that I don't know how to say it,
it's that I don't think I can do it without crying.
And maybe that's the point—
because you know me well enough to know
that I've never been good with words,
only with feeling.

But I need you to know,
in the silence that exists between us,
that I'm thankful.
More than you'll ever know.

I haven't said thank you because we're too gay for that shit

Outside Looking In

Outside looking in, I know what it looks like—
It seems like I didn't care,
Like I didn't consider the monumental effect
This would have on the people in my life.
From the outside, I know I seem selfish and weak.
Maybe I am.

Disney taught me to wait for my Prince Charming to save me,
While society insisted that *it* wasn't the answer.
I grew tired of waiting,
Tired of hoping,
Tired of fighting.

Outside looking in, they think they know,
But they can't see the battles I fight in silence,
The weight I carry,
The exhaustion that settles deep in my bones.
I got tired of searching for answers,
So I made one,
A choice that seemed like the only escape,
Societal norms be damned.

Trusted Adult

I remember being taught in school:
"Go to a trusted adult."
But no one tells you what to do
When that trusted adult is the one
Who turns your trust into a weapon.

What they don't teach you
Is how to survive when trust
Becomes the knife they twist in your back.

You were supposed to protect me.
Instead, you taught me to tread lightly,
To scan your face for cracks in your kindness,
To tiptoe around your moods,
Careful not to offer ammunition.

My moments of weakness
Shouldn't have been the weapon you wielded,
The tool you sharpened
To carve out control.

But you did.
Every time I cried,
You made it about you
Every fear I confided
Became another leash
Pulled tighter when I dared to question.

You told me I was selfish
For needing space.
Ungrateful,
When I couldn't meet your impossible standards—
The ones you swore were for my own good.

You were my mother.
My trusted adult.
But I was never safe with you.0

You bent me until I couldn't see
Where you ended and I began.
You held my secrets like fire—
Not to warm me,
But to scorch me when I stepped out of line.

Now your voice echoes in my head,
Telling me I'm not enough,
Not worthy,
Unless I'm exactly what you want me to be.

How do I unlearn this guilt?
How do I stop the instinct
To brace myself around those I love?

You taught me that trust is fragile,
That sometimes the ones we're told to lean on
Are the ones who will break us.

So tell me—
What am I supposed to do now?
Who do I go to
When the person I trusted most
Taught me that trust can destroy?

I'm Okay

I'm okay.
I have to be.
Because no one else will stop the world
Long enough for me to breathe
And simply not be

V. Whispers of
Everday Life

Moments of reflection on life's small joys and fleeting moments

I Love a Rainy Day

I love a rainy or stormy day;
I find beauty in the dark sky.
I find solace in the raindrops that fall,
For they remind me I'm not the only one that cries.
The sky weeps too,
And she's so beautiful when she does,
So perhaps it's okay that I do too.

Living in the Moment

Memories fade,
but feelings linger—
sharp, stubborn things
that refuse to let go.

So let's hold this moment,
freeze it in time,
before it slips through our fingers
like the others did.

Because I'm tired—
tired of chasing shadows,
tired of living in the past,
tired of carrying ghosts
that don't know when to leave.

Let this be the one
I don't have to run from.

A Nightly Resolution

I pay homage to each star
That has witnessed the tears I've shed,
And to the stars that have seen
More than they ever should.

No matter how the story unfolds,
I will rest in the knowledge
That I lived—
And in that living,
I found peace.

Painted Smile

I have a painted smile,
Drawn with permanent marker and sealed with ink.
It's not going anywhere,
This painted smile of mine.
It's useful—
It hides my pain.

It's the mask I wear every day,
Practiced and easy to maintain.
It hides the tears I shed each night,
As I whisper, "I'm okay."
I hide behind this painted smile,
But beneath it, I'm breaking.

Hidden

I want to be a work of art,
Framed and hung up on your wall,
Something you'd be proud to call your own.
But all I ever was
Was a hidden, dirty secret,
Tucked away in a box in the closet.

Appreciation

I want to see myself
from a point of view
where I can fall in love with who I am—
not with a critical eye,
always analyzing
the things I lack,
the flaws that echo louder than my virtues,
but with eyes that soften,
that linger on the good,
that appreciate all that I have,
all that I am,
and all that I am becoming.

Gotta start somewhere

To Be Written

For once, I wish to be
the story, not the storyteller.
To be the one the words are about,
not the one giving them life.

Oh, to be the poem—
to rest in the lines,
to be felt, not shaped.
To be seen without having to explain,
without the weight of my own hand.

I long for the quiet of being the ink,
not the hand that holds the pen.
To be the voice that speaks,
not the one who must first find it.

Not Yet

I'll be honest—
I don't want to be alive right now.
I wanted to lie beside you,
to let the dirt cover me too,
to end the ache that screams in your absence.

What's the point of standing
when every breath feels hollow?
What's the point of moving
when the world moves on without you in it?

There are moments I find myself
staring into the abyss,
wondering if the weight would lift
if I just gave in.
The thought tempts me—
whispers that peace waits beneath the soil.

But then I think about you.
About the life you poured into me.
The sacrifices,
the love,
the battles you fought so I wouldn't have to.

To die now would erase everything you built.
It would waste the years you spent
shaping me into someone you believed in.
And I cherish that too much
to let it slip into the void.

Your legacy dies with me, and I'm not ready to end it.
Not yet.

Judgement

When the world called me strange,
I buckled under the weight of their words,
But now I stand tall, unbroken.
Why I buckled can be traced to my desire to be wanted, needed,
to be normal.
One could argue, "Is the world really normal?"
But within the standards and rules we live by, it could be
considered our normal.

I faltered beneath their glare and judgment,
Wincing with every breath and step as I continued to be me.
I ache beneath the strain,
Shudder beneath the weight,
And each night, I pant and cry from the pain.

If I could tell you now the words I wished to say then,
Would you see me differently—
or judge me still?
If I told you how I ache for a sliver of hope, a chance,
Would you hold me, say we could start again?

For you see, I am me and will continue to be,
But that does not mean I don't shudder beneath your steely gaze.
I am a woman of many shades, many sides, many names,
But beneath all that lies one claim:
I ache all over. For what? I am not sure.
Perhaps it's closure, or a life I've only ever dreamed of—
a dream I cannot touch without aching.

I ache for acceptance, for solace not yet found,
A yearning too deep to be named.
I ache for the shame that lingers,
Knowing the fate of the world lies at our fingers.
I ache knowing that with such immense power, we know not what we do.
We're a mess, yet in an odd way, someone's dream come true.
We are innovators and thinkers, dreamers and creators.
We are our own damnation.
Should we take comfort in that? Should I?

That the world, our life, my life, is covered in gray,
Because uncertainty is all we know.
Nothing is solid. Nothing is set in stone.
But I do know that when the world called me strange,
I buckled under the weight of their words,
Sighing softly without a single word.

Strange, perhaps, but then again, so are you.
I buckled, yes, but now I stand like roots in the storm.

Yellow

Who's your yellow? They asked
"I am" I replied
I saved myself for no one else dared to

Warped Image

A shattered image in the glass,
But the mirror's not broken—
only my perception of myself.
I gaze, the surface whole,
Yet inside, I crack and crumble,
A fracture that won't heal,
Splintering deeper with each passing day.

Insecurities bind me tight,
And the mirror reflects my plight.

Shattered Reflection

Sometimes, I stare at my reflection,
searching the emptiness in my eyes,
the void in my soul,
the marks on my skin, the expression on my face.

I trace the stretch marks,
the scars that litter me,
etched across my body and soul.
I examine my bleeding heart,
bruised, black-and-blue,
bearing the words left unsaid,
the wounds unresolved,
my cowardice, my self-hatred.

I wonder if this will ever change.
But to change it, I must first change.
And I don't know if I can,
in a world that feels so suffocating.

Sometimes, I just stare,
watching sadness coil around me,
seeing the child inside, still broken,
her bloodshot eyes, the tears that never stop.
I want to console her, but I don't know how.
I want to tell her it gets better,
but I can't promise that.

I see her pleading,
and I break,
because I have no answers to give.
I stare at my imperfections,
wondering why I can't love them,

why I can't love myself.
I trace each blemish,
and wonder what it would feel like
to fall in love with the person I see.

Would it change me?
Would it set me free?
I look at the woman in the mirror,
and I realize I don't recognize her.
She's a stranger,
fractured in the cracked glass.

I see the red, the scars,
the emptiness.
The broken pieces,
the unforgivable vengeance.
I stare, and I cry.
I cry until there's nothing left.

It hurts.
My body hurts.
My head hurts.
Everything hurts.

Please, make it stop.
I'm not strong enough.
I can't take it.
I was never enough.
Please, make it stop.

I look down.
A blade is in my hand.
I don't know how it got there.
I watch as I drag it across my skin,
across my heart,
cutting, hurting,
killing the vessel
because that's all it's ever been.

No one is living here anymore.
The spirit died long ago.
The heart stopped beating years ago.
Hope stopped hoping ages ago.
The mind stopped thinking long ago.

I stare and stare.
I hate what I see.

Nights Like These

On nights like these, I question everything—
The point of it all,
The purpose of this weight I carry,
The reason for the ache in my chest.
On nights like these,
When tears fall uninvited,
And I've been smothered once again,
I question who I am.
I feel hollow, as if everything I once had
Has been quietly stripped away.
On nights like these,
I can't tell if I hate myself,
Or if it's just life
That I can't bear.

The Things I Am

Joker said it best:
"I am not someone who is loved. I am an idea. A state of mind."

I am a placeholder,
A fleeting warmth,
Treated like every desperate, broken thought
You've ever conjured into reality.

I am not someone who is loved.
I am an idea,
A passing desire,
A fantasy too dangerous to keep.

A thrill,
I am the demon you entertain in the dark,
The cigarette you crave,
Then discard once the taste fades.
The blunt you hide,
When red and blue flash by,
The drink you can't resist—
One more,
To dull the ache,
Because in your tortured, alcohol-fogged mind,
I'm the cure for your pain.

I am not someone who is loved.
I am an idea.
I am the side chick,
Good enough to satisfy,
But never worthy of being brought home.

I am the one who matches every desire,
Every secret wish you'd rather keep hidden,
Like smoke curling away into the night.

I am not someone who is loved.
I am just an idea—
A temporary indulgence,
A fleeting escape.

In Another Universe

In another universe,
I am not shattered glass,
Fragile in the wrong hands
And sharp enough to cut my own.

There, my mind isn't a maze
Of doubts and regrets,
A broken record of "what ifs"
Scratching at the edges of my peace.

In that world,
I don't flinch at my reflection,
Don't brace myself for the voices
That sound too much like my own.

Scars are just stories,
Not heavy chains.
The weight I carry is light—
Just enough to remind me
Of what I've overcome,
Not what I've lost.

In another universe,
I know what it feels
like To wake up whole.
To take a breath
And not feel it catch
On the shards of my past.

In that place,
I am soft and steady,
Unburdened by the need to fight
Every second of the day.

And maybe there,
I don't wish for escape.
Maybe there,
I look in the mirror and see
Someone worth staying for.

But here?
Here I am still piecing myself together,
Still learning how to hold my broken parts
Without bleeding.

And maybe one day,
This universe will feel like enough

AM Ramblings

On nights when thoughts keep me awake,
The world is a door I cannot open,
Its answers suffocating beneath my chest.
The moonlight slips through the window,
Chasing the shadows in the room—
A light I wish could chase the darkness inside me.

Am I complacent? Maybe. Restless? Certainly.
I toss beneath sheets,
Gripped by a search for peace
That's always just out of reach.
Not here, not in this prison
I've built from my own mind.

What do I want from life?
I draw a blank, yet something stirs—
A whisper I almost understand:
I want to help.
To help those who need it,
And maybe, to help myself.
But isn't that everyone's answer?
What do I want? I'm not sure.
But I want peace. I want happiness—
For me, this time.

The path will be hard,
I know that.
But I'm okay with it—
The best things are never easy.
Ironic, isn't it?
Slumber calls to my tired body,
A familiar battle of mind versus flesh.

In the stillness,
I can only write—
The words of a restless mind
No one will ever understand.

My Bittersweet Feelings

Sometimes the tears fall before I can catch them.
They fall before I feel them.
They fall and fall and fall.
Each tear is a word,
A feeling,
A glimpse into the inside.

One tear: I ache.
Two tears: the pain.
Three tears: I'm sorry.
Four tears: I'm broken, a soul shaken.

Sometimes the tears fall before I can catch them.
They're quiet and shy,
Each one a glimpse into my soul.
They fall and fall,
Caught only by the fabric of my clothes.

But I envy them.
Yes, I do, because while they fall hot and fast,
They have something to catch them,
Something to absorb their pain and grief.
When I fell, I fell hard
Then shattered on the pavement,
Pieces flying—
Never to be recovered.

Fools

Now they'll sit there, staring at my casket,
Crying tears that won't save me—
Fools, all of them.

VI. Seeking Meaning

Exploring existential and spiritual questions about life, faith, and purpose.

Adulting

Man, adulting sucks
Who authorized this shit?

Questioning Faith

It's strange how religion weaves through my grief.
I grew up believing in a perfect God,
an entity incapable of wrong.
But as the years passed, my certainty cracked,
and I found myself questioning all I'd been taught.

The Epicurean paradox echoes in my mind:
"Is God willing to prevent evil, but not able? Then He is not omnipotent.
Is He able, but not willing? Then He is malevolent.
Is He both able and willing? Then whence cometh evil?
Is He neither able nor willing? Then why call Him God?"

If He knows all,
then this pain I carry was scripted long before,
and that feels cruel.

And I'm not sure I can convince myself
that the being I might have faith in is that cruel.
Does that make Him a cruel God?
Or perhaps He isn't cruel at all.
What if there is no God?
What if He is nothing more
than an idea, a figurehead
we've placed on a pedestal,
who's forgotten the chaos of our lives?

Or maybe He's not cruel at all.
Perhaps this is simply life.
Maybe this was His plan,
for reasons beyond me,
but through my human eyes,
it seems cruel, childishly unfair.

I question my faith. I question Him.
Answers I do not have.
So I don't know. But the questions remain,
and I wish I had the answers.

What I do know is this:
You weren't perfect, but you tried. You were good.
There are worse people He could have taken,
if this was truly His doing.

So I'm supposed to honor a God
who shattered my world in a blink?
That doesn't sit right with me.
I call bullshit.
Yes, I know I'm being petty. Sue me.

Failure's Weight

I don't think the concept of failure hurts;
I think it's the weight of its knowledge that stings—
The understanding that if we fail,
We let down everyone who believed in us,
Who placed their hope in us,
Who invested in us,
And cheered us on.
Is that why I feel this failure so acutely?
I wish you were here to tell me I shouldn't feel this way.
You died. I died. Our plans died.
It feels like all the hard work you put in was for naught—
A truly miserable feeling.

When the Past Starts Calling

Whispers linger,
Shadows of forgotten moments,
Pulling me back into the pain.
Memories, once buried,
Shake off the dust of neglect,
Rising with a whirlwind of anguish.

The child within me cowers,
Her voice trembling in silent pleas,
Crying tears she was once too strong to shed.

I feel the weight of my demons,
Their whispers growing louder,
Their shadows stretching longer.
I fight, but the darkness deepens,
And I fear I'm losing—
A battle against shadows I cannot outrun.

Lie

My therapist always asks,
"How was your anxiety this week?"
I always say,
"It's been okay."

But I don't tell her
How it's suffocating,
Paralyzing,
A quiet war I'm losing in my chest.
Her tools don't work,
But I nod anyway,
Playing along—
Yeah, I know,
I'm a liar.

A Continuation

Atticus once wrote:
"Never go in search of love;
Go in search of life,
And life will find you
And the love you seek."

And when it does,
You'll learn to live for love,
And love to live.
You'll find joy in the mundane,
And beauty in the broken.

A Drunk Mind Meets a Sober Heart

I sat down with my third? Fourth? Sixth drink of the night,
Vision blurry, hands trembling, and with a
Face streaked with tears as I looked to the night sky—
A sky more midnight blue than black,
Glittering with billions of stars,
Each burning hot with purpose,
While I sat, cold and empty,
On the cool, damp grass, lost in my own abyss.

And then, in a rush,
My mouth opened,
And I cried—
Cried until my chest ached,
Until my lungs burned,
Until I couldn't tell if I was breaking apart or coming undone.

I was drunk.
My mind stumbling over itself.
Each thought heavier than the last,
Desperate to drown in the liquor's embrace.

But my heart—poor, stubborn thing—
She was sober. She could not escape the weight,
Could not dull the ache.
So she screamed,
Fury and grief pouring from her like waves
Crashing against a shore no one stood on.

The tragedy was,
There was no one to hear her wail,
No witness to her pain.
And so I sat there—drunk, ruined—
Mind and body numbing themselves together,
While my heart, quiet and raw,
Held every shard of my breaking.

It was in that moment—
When the drunk mind stumbled and fell
Into the arms of the sober heart—
That I realized the truth.
The heart cannot drink to forget.
The mind cannot cry itself whole.
And together, they will always meet
In the wreckage of what was,
Trying to hold each other up,
Even as they both break apart.

So I sat there,
Under a sky that burned with purpose,
Drunk in body,
Sober in soul,
And accepted that some pains
Cannot be drowned.

A drunk mind and a sober heart meet again